MIT●CHONDRIAL NIGHT

ALSO BY ED BOK LEE

Real Karaoke People
Whorled

MIT●CHONDRIAL NIGHT

ED BOK LEE

COFFEE HOUSE PRESS

Minneapolis

2019

Coffee House Press books are available to the trade through our primary distributor, Consortium Book Sales & Distribution, cbsd.com or (800) 283-3572. For personal orders, catalogs, or other information, write to info@coffeehousepress.org.

Coffee House Press is a nonprofit literary publishing house. Support from private foundations, corporate giving programs, government programs, and generous individuals helps make the publication of our books possible. We gratefully acknowledge their support in detail in the back of this book.

LIBRARY OF CONGRESS CATALOGING-IN-PUBLICATION DATA

Names: Lee, Ed Bok, author.
Title: Mitochondrial night / Ed Bok Lee.
Description: Minneapolis : Coffee House Press, [2019]
Identifiers: LCCN 2018038608 (print) | LCCN 2018038841 (ebook) |
    ISBN 9781566895415 | ISBN 9781566895323 (trade pbk.)
Classification: LCC PS3612.E34277 (ebook) | LCC PS3612.E34277 A6 2019
    (print) | DDC 811/.6—dc23
LC record available at https://lccn.loc.gov/2018038608

ACKNOWLEDGMENTS

Gratitude to each of the editors and curators of the following publications and exhibitions for first selecting or commissioning many of the poems in this collection, sometimes in earlier versions: *Hayden's Ferry Review,* Academy of American Poets (www.poets.org), *Fence, Tupelo Quarterly, VOLT, Gulf Coast, Diode, Missouri Review, Copper Nickel, Water~Stone Review, Hawai'i Pacific Review, Sleet Magazine, Conduit,* the *Apple Valley Review, Mizna, LUMINA,* Poetry and Pie, the Pillsbury House Art Block series, *Tinderbox Poetry Journal,* Coffee House Press *Books in Action*/American Swedish Institute, *Revolver, Into Quarterly, We/Here, Left Hooks, Razor,* and the *Normal School.*

Thank you to my family, friends, and fellow writers and artists. Special thanks to Susan Solomon, Kale Yu, Alison McGhee, Kathryn Haddad, Tom Welsford, Wei-li Yeh, Molly Van Avery, Bridget Mendel, and Idouna Lee. Much appreciation also to the Minnesota State Arts Board Artist Initiative grant, Chris Fischbach, Erika Stevens, Carla Valadez, and everyone at Coffee House Press.

어머님께

CONTENTS

III. COLONIZING A DIFFERENT SUN

MIT●CHONDRIAL NIGHT

RANDOM FLOATING CELLS WITH STYLE

To love one another with quantum certainty is to volumize the stars.

It might take some time, a few million years, but for your efforts—
    many more

moth-white, fuzzy, brightened blurs. There, someone

once upon a time loved despite. There, another

just shed enough fears in love not to burst. Each evening,

this movie of love plays out like popcorn blinking lively in the sky.

As if your epilogue were an ancient, omniscient satellite to whom

time no longer matters, and matter always exceeds the count.

Ah, you bonus illumination in this vast multiplying apart.

You gathering of random floating cells with style.

You—all of you—dying trillions of times every hour

to recommence each new forever inside these eyes. Look.

Look at me seeing you seeing me from the beginning of the universe
    and time.

Never forget: wherever, whenever you are, is the history of all you loved
    in the dark.

ULTRAVI●LET CITY

METAPHORMOSIS

"Omnia mutantur, nihil interit."
—OVID, *METAMORPHOSES*

The Hohokam people of what is now Arizona abruptly left corn in bowls on tables in their mountain cave pueblos; abandoned even their clothes and ladders for reasons unknown.

The Çatalhöyük mysteriously deserted polished obsidian mirrors, worked-bone buckles and rings, and countless other belongings inside the system of mud-brick and timber hives they built overlooking the Konya Plain of now south-central Turkey nine thousand years ago.

Last year, my seventy-seven-year-old mother forgot for two days where she parked her car.

On the rare occasions she gives in to my coaxing and speaks of what is now North Korea, accentuating her childhood dialect, I'm reminded of the many nations that have come and gone—been renamed, reclassified, rebordered, even in my own lifetime—Burma, u.s.s.r., Ceylon, etcetera. The other day I heard the Czech Republic, formerly of Czechoslovakia, and before that the Czechoslovak Republic, preceded by Bohemia, has now officially become Czechia.

If you go back long enough, Ethiopia reverts to Abyssinia, Iran to Persia, Algeria refills with Numidians, in Libya there is a Cyrenaican queen, and so on.

This natural shifting of classifications has some interesting ontological implications. Once, when my mother—unconsciously in the voice of an old auntie—was recollecting traditional methods for cultivating perilla leaves and gourds, the long-dead woman's husky mannerisms and speech referred in passing to practices and techniques not of Korea, or Corea, or North Korea, but Chosun, which forced a hiccup in my mother's recollection, a pause from the living dream she was translating—in her effort now to explain in more somber English, the history of the ever-shifting nomenclature and borders of her homeland, for the sake of my wife and friends.

Eventually, my mother recommenced her account of her early adventures as a child gardening for hobby, then supplement, and finally for survival during and after a war that, overnight, invalidated her passport—though her colorful, unconscious portrayal of the old auntie's playful tones and animated gestures that had made the story so fun, had inflected the worldview, never did fully return.

Mitochondria, energy-producing organelles in our cells, inherited exclusively from one's mother/maternal line ad infinitum, derives its name from the modern Latin, which derives from the Greek *mitos* "thread" and *khondrion* "granule," "grain," or "morsel." In Sami, *word* also means "trap." In Russian, *vodka* means "little water." Now I'm thinking of other nomenclature, gestures, concepts, tones, attitudes, styles—all the modes of consciousness we've imbibed and exhaled over eons in our ongoing necessity to translate this mysterious Poem of Life into prose.

Recently I caught my mother staring at my newborn daughter as I rocked her in my arms. The question going around the living room in my mother's condo was whether our five-week-old was truly smiling at me, could register joy, let alone discern between different faces and voices . . . or was just passing gas.

"I was reading it's just one big blur at this point," muttered Bridget, the most exhausted of all, setting down her sketch pad before taking a sip of lemon-and-mint water.

Suddenly I noticed my mother chopping garlic in the kitchen, flying around the room, darning her blazer, driving me to nursery school, gluing a celadon vase . . . and in every other place I could recall simultaneously, in one intense profusion.

"A blur of lights and whooshes of sound to her brand-new senses," Bridget continued, "so that ten days to a baby her age, relative to her time on earth, would feel to any of us like a quarter of our lifetimes."

I remember thinking maybe it's not that the memory of old people fails, but that each moment happens in such thinner fractions of total earthly recollection—if they blink too slowly, whole nations and kingdoms come and are gone.

The next day, we three flew home, high above several increasingly newer states, at once forward and backward in time.

HALFWAY TO A NEW HOME

—for my mother

After the coal train emerged from yet another tunnel, hissing
to still for a hundred more war refugees along a blue, snow-crusted road
    between Seoul & Busan

your father climbed down & carried your lifeless brother into the woods.

Your little hands still purple
from earlier piggybacking his toddler limbs & feverish moans to the station
    as if handcuffed alone in prayer.

Tracks years narrower than the roads from Taiyuan to Sinuiju to Pyeongyang
    to Incheon when you were two, then four, then six years old,

yourself first swaddled under stars
by an auntie who later drowned in the Taedong River when the communists
    declared victory in the North.

✻

At a Marathon station midway to Florida,
I sit & take the wheel while you retune the radio then recline your seat—

A report on the latest casualties in Syria, Afghanistan, Iraq, in Bosnia, East
    Timor, Chechnya, Palestine, the Congo, Guatemala—

Don't fall asleep, you mumble, eyes closed, to me, your only son.

✻

Of the dead farmer you saw frozen like a scarecrow in a cornfield outside
    Sariwon, his long black coat a tent still protecting his three weeping
    children—

Of the high-pitched rocket you witnessed gore a woman's torso in a roofless
    church—

Of the scrunch of passing tanks, far tremolo of mortars, bullets shattering
    the January air like the spectacles illiterate soldiers plucked off your
    grandfather's nose, grinding the glass into floorboards your brothers
    and uncles waited beneath, like tubers growing hair—

Of all the orphans & famished travelers, war after war, road after road—

This sleek black asphalt on a gray-lit Wednesday
must feel like an epilogue,
a coda, a bonus track about an elderly Korean woman traveling to her new,
    final home—seven decades later

along a winding road through the Great Smokies of Georgia, tracking
endless dash marks like minus signs, or breadcrumbs, or the overgrown
    femurs of ghosts & angels.

*

At dusk, a cloud approaches, curious of us.

I switch off the hip-hop station & listen to you softly snore.

Far in the rearview mirror, an invisible boy lights a match across the horizon

entreating even the plainest coffin of ash

or zelkova or maple & birch trees dipping & rising all the way to the Taebaek
    Mountains to cradle him warm.

*

A high wind rouses our car & trailer

until every confiscated diamond in the night has returned every lost love letter.

PLAYHOUSE

A man is binding a rooftop
he's thatched together in dreams
from thousands of fallen strands of hair

his mother, wife, and daughter
have thus far left behind. Now
that their little girl can say a few words

(and points at halos above certain foreheads),
his aim is to construct a sanctuary
where the child can play, hide, or just laze all July—

imagining, reenacting, singing
to make-believe tea and a backyard breeze.
His very old mother has lately flown in from far away.

His very young daughter has come
from an even farther place within his wife
who is now catching up with her own mother, both laughing

harmonizing, reverberating
on phones in separate living rooms states apart.
The little hut the man

is busy canopying with fallen strands of hair
his mother, wife, and daughter
have thus far left behind

will be both
primitive and futuristic:
part wood, grass, plastic

castle, spaceship, cocoon, and cathedral
of double helixes, left unlocked
in this shade-dappled corner of the universe

amid peach and oak,
heaven and earth,
water and fire—for anything

with or without wings
seeking shelter from the eternity inside us all.

ULTRAVIOLET SHAMAN

"A ritual must be passed through with the whole body ..."
—JANE HIRSHFIELD

Stop, says Seonsengnim, my drum
teacher in Seoul, tapping my wrist
with his yeolchae stick, not hard
as when I was a boy in Mapo
and my tae kwon do instructor bruised
with nunchucks my supinate palms
for fighting at school.
                              *Remember, this drum
is a horse you're galloping ... Now, loosen up, and start again.*
Seonsengnim is white haired,
formerly homeless, until a troupe
of much younger drummers found him
in his fifty-eighth year sleeping in a park
and taught him seoljanggu—its ancient
cadences for thirty centuries, which now
he teaches beginners for a pittance. I observe
he crashes in this, their jerry-rigged
drumming studio in Edae, on the linoleum
beside a portable gas burner he places
a copper kettle atop as a makeshift humidifier.
He sips barley tea until the sun goes down
and a soju bottle comes out. *Here, drink this
to oil the soul warm.*
                              He has one student, me,
and a lazy eye, a weak gray mustache, and little education.
Soju, it helps you understand the horse. His father,
an infantryman, froze to death during the war,
and his mother disappeared when he was six, maybe escaped
or was kidnapped back to the North.
Now just another old man
with no friends and a childlike smile you see
wandering the streets of Seoul.
All right, that's enough for today, the horse is tired.
On Friday mornings he drum-dances solo

at orphanages and elderly centers: a cantering
dervish on horsehide and deerskin heads
stretched over hourglass-
shaped paulownia wood; the deep
and simultaneous staccato rhythms long and intricate
enough to harken the Neolithic.
Drum patterns I keep forgetting
when I play as if tracking animals
on a damp trail through mountain mist.
Drifting off each night five subway stops away,
I strain to memorize them, tapping out long
segments against my thighs in my jachwi room, rented
usually by the week for test preparation.
There is coarse mothball bedding; a communal
shower that whines and sprays only ice water; and a flickering
fluorescent tube over a study carrel
in what can only be described as a cell.
Law exams. College entrance exams. Medical school
exams. Police exams. Realtor exams. The occupants
sigh and groan and fart through the walls,
stretch stiff limbs in the halls,
are generally testy in this stressed-
out land, highest suicide rate in the developed world.
Seoul.
          You, city where my earliest memories surge
into tanks cracking asphalt, sirens, martial
law over bullhorns, protests
and tear gas each week on my way to kindergarten.
A South Korean military dictator who imprisoned and beat
poets like drums
until brain damaged into honorary jobs
in the propaganda department.
Seoul. You, history of mortars
and rockets like monstrous shovels
exhuming ancestral bones.
                    I have returned
to renovate my heart with a million
precolonial kidak strokes and pulsating googoongs.

Stored up all my belongings
in Brooklyn, sold my rusted Mercury,
and arrived to beat whatever I need
out of both you and me,
twelve hours a day. Sometimes
we skip meals and pound on, lost
in the DNA-yoke of powerful tempos.

On Sundays,
the studio's professional crew comes
and together we all touch knees and shoulders
and drum
an invisible history reanimating the guttural chants
of priests and rice farmers.
Themes and variations long ago
invented to help defeat
the stooping tedium and uncertainty
of seedlings in tempestuous fields; so the back-
bone doesn't crack and seep
like the milky broth of oxtails and noodles
some nights we go around the corner to slurp
together, this old man and me,
in sweat-soaked shirts.
He will die in six years.
He will wheeze through a cancerous lung,
his one good eye gone fishy dim.
But, I hear, he sat and drummed till the end.

Often I go for months
without thinking of him; that winter
into spring; those few cherry blossom
branches quicker to bloom
for their proximity to a train line.
The walls where I live now
are all too thin, so
if I must, I drive to my office
in Saint Paul at night to thunder shit out.
When the way won't come.
And the dead shapes shine.
I drum

and think of the old, galloping Korean
who, one night over dried squid and beer,
confided he didn't play for the small
studio's leaky roof over his head.
He preferred bridges. Did not play
for the meager wage. Understood
the troupe's leaders only assigned him
the random hobbyists passing through.
He knew he began the art way too late.
And that his hands would sometimes shake.
And he took too many smoke breaks.
He played, he claimed,
for other reasons: spiritual but not
as prayer like all the churches
that ever fed and took him in
waited for him to do. Not for repentance
or supplication or sublime escape
or even meditation.
                    We're drumming,
he explained, in the tradition
of shamans,
so the ancestors won't be so lonely.
Because the spirits need us
more than we need them.
And for hours
                they'll listen to anyone.

POWDERHORN

Cowbell wind chimes clang
In this quiet pocket of the city.

Lesbians love living here.
Brutalized philosophers

Of color. Pit bull walkers. Exiles.
Immigrants. Jugglers. Where

Grizzly hippies spill coffee
Over the Crisis of Capitalism,

Apiary priests pray to their bees, and hydra-
Headed emcees slowly go gray.

Kingdom of nightshade, weeping
Willow, and concrete. City

Lake cosmos of nighttime
Stars wheeling a young

Boy's trowel in a front yard carrot patch
Sunday mornings beside tattoo-faced parents

On their hands and knees, weeding.
Toddler to the knowledge

That the world redesigned by yet another
Solar system in another galaxy begins

With each Glock's shot in the distance. Sirens
Sing their far syllables of sin and lament. Crack, smack, and sex

Workers shuffling subzero steps at the perimeter like puff-
Hooded sentinels, all winter into spring's

Newest chicks, pecking, clucking
Through broken vodka bottles and dandelions.

Midwest, Midtown
Contiguity of the future and past;

Part metropolis,
Part grassland.

Sunday fútbol in Somali-slurred Spanish,
Pagan puppet street parade each May,

And Mike Hoyt's tri-ped portable karaoke
Projecting lyrics on a Greenway underpass

For punks, bankers, activists, nurses—anyone
On a summer Saturday night who brakes and croons

Before biking on. Meanwhile,
Lowriders shimmy. Native teens

In saggy pants glare or clown
By the monkey bars. Cops like orcas

Troll. And brothers brawl
With chain mail, ballet, and a basketball.

Once upon a time, the world longed
For milk, so the sun touched its aching tusks

To the moon's boiling door
To borrow a little soil, a little cloud,

Until old worms tunneled into new bones.
Meanwhile, the deer-dreaming wind spread seeds

And ashes over the earth. Snow
Soon joined in. Mulberry

Wine inside larks. All sky art. Pond-
Stewed ions. Humans. Meditation. Poetry. Shit,

I almost forgot—Chonny's Bhangra Basement Barbeque
Each Friday at sunset

For *anyone* who wants to get down
And churn

Their own color across this canvas.

HIPPARCHUS'S MOTHER ON LOVE,
STARS & TRANSMUTATION

Look for someone who stares
From the dark beyond stars
When caressing each other's voices
Even on the phone

You are newly a man
And don't yet know how to see
But others in mirrors
Seeing you seeing them
Myriad millennia ago

Trapped,
Twirling
Inside your freedom

BALLAD OF THE PRETTY GOOD

—for J. K.

A pretty good friend came back from warring, as men have done since fire and families, and shot himself in the heart with a SIG Sauer. The note he left instructed his sister to donate his brain to Parkinson's research, his kidneys to a Muslim or two in need, his pancreas to cancer, and his eyes to diabetes. The contents of his bank account he gave to his sister and her children's college fund.

He was all-American, wheat-haired, played football and hockey. He did possess a dark side, but pretty openly on social media. He'd cheated on his wife when married, gambled and drunk too much, frequented strip clubs. But he got himself back into shape, over a decade after fighting in the first Gulf War, and reenlisted to go to Iraq. Here is where the summation of his life becomes heroic or tragic. Here is where America will comprise the storm troopers or Jedis. I offer the following account for future historians to assess in our long and rightful chapter within the Book of Nations.

The caretaker of the shabby studio apartment where the suicide happened was not a very good friend of mine or the departed's. This not-very-good friend had been letting my pretty good friend basically squat there for a few months, while the latter got back on his feet. I had no idea they'd reconnected as grown men. We all used to ride our bikes to the river in grade school, hunting turtles with sticks and shooting sparrows with slingshots. Borrowed gutters directed our bottle rockets in a warped game of combat tag. My pretty good friend was always in charge. The not-very-good friend, I think, felt fortunate just to be allowed to follow our dirt bikes around on his sister's rickety ten-speed. His father was a divorced Vietnam vet and alcoholic. The kid lived on snack cakes, soft bread, and bologna. And then like autumn trees we three fluttered orange, yellow, red, off in our own directions into middle and high school and towns beyond.

I saw that one not-very-good friend again four years after my pretty good friend's suicide. This stooped, lanky man somehow recognized me in a grocery parking lot while carrying his two-year-old daughter, who sucked on a blue popsicle. He spoke openly with odd amazement of the mess left on the white wall and carpet in the apartment he'd let our mutual friend squat in.

There was splattered blood and a curious, watermelon seed–sized bit of hardened flesh that he'd found lodged in the hollow of a window frame that the painters had missed. He spoke openly of how he'd momentarily debated whether or not to call someone about the dry, plum-colored speck of what he thought was *probably heart matter.*

Now his little girl wriggled in his arms. He released her onto the hot asphalt, also lowering his voice in speaking of how stressful it was for him as the building's caretaker whenever the infamous unit went vacant and he had to start showing it again. In the end, this not-very-good friend wrapped the bit of *probably heart matter* in a plastic baggie and stored it in his freezer. As we strolled to, then stopped beside my car, he confessed that, though he'd never really liked the departed, who'd always picked on his poverty and difference, he'd kept it. "Just in case science ever comes up with a way to bring back the dead." He said this smiling, nervous, strange as ever. And then I got into my car with my carrots and eggs, and remembered how, whenever he was around, my pretty good friend and I never fought.

THE DESERT VS. THE SEA

Tonight you can hear the desert and sea
arguing again. The old desert keeps
demanding to know who stripped all its green.
The ghost sea can only spray more sand
and weep.

Did you know, in any version of eternity,
you can send back the heart you are
presently scheduled to depart with when old?
Just erase any trace of who you think you should be.

Fuller than all futures
were to you as a child, the heart I mean
doesn't care if it houses a body.

And not any prophet's heart by proxy;
but a heart that returns from a long journey of its own, widened
like hips or jowls; fed in the sweet
orchard of attempts and regrets;
a heart that can finally receive but doesn't need
what it loves to give.

Like those freest birds who chirp at the zoo,
alighting with snippets of news
for the lumbering hearts long blind behind rusted bars and grids of wire.

In the desert, they arrive onto a cholla—
candy-blue wings and fast clicks
warning the quail, who warn the jackrabbits,
who inform the squirrels of a snake's or coyote's sultry approach.

And afterward, with softening notes
from such small-plumed throats,
they linger to chirp old tales of

plankton and whales.

SCHOOL KILLED BY PAPER GUN SHOOTING SUGAR

When fire was mastered, amateur sinners
turned professional overnight.

Wild olives in the mouths of ruminants
soon oiled the human voice.

At this rate, it's only a matter of time
before E. coli in bifocals snip-snip

our genes like Christmas ribbons.
Already, I swear after hearing only three words

I can smell the wattage of light bulb
used to compose any speech

by any world leader's chuckling scriptwriters.
And no mausoleum in a pundit's mouth

merits all the rat traps & chemicals. America,
we're not going back to Saturday cowboy

matinees & milk on stoops. You can try
pressing your head into a more

consistent dream like lately the one
I've had of sentient kerosene

lamps floating through a pitch-black museum
in search of their blue whale ancestors.

All I know: the God Lamp above
all this seawater in our cells

dresses its outermost simulacra
in vanity, now regret, now melancholy, joy,

now awe, anticipation, now distraction
like tonight the sitar across our alley is warming

up with Tunisian airline jingles.
At its core: a song about a life

so imperfect it hurts to feel
the beauty that holds all the shards

together. The old me in my expired
passport already apparently knows: when my daughter

is my age, she will ask why, like meth, we
didn't then regulate gunpowder?

I may only be alive via hologram
on shuffle. So, Babygirl, tonight

as I write, the quarter moon shines
yellow as a Soviet sickle bat signal.

It reminds me of the tale your grandmother tells
of how as a girl in North Korea one spring

they announced an emergency ration
on all adjectives & verbs.

No one cared. Nouns were simpler.
And the next day free cotton candy

spun by an old man on a stationary bicycle
was handed out like bouquets, coned

inside newspapers full of
faded images & no more words.

AMERICAN MEN

Walid says he's working overtime to keep his eleven-year-old son in an elite private middle school; doesn't want the kid painted too "colored" or Muslim when he's an adult; wants him to know the "American heart" better than it knows itself.

I take a sip of beer & glance at another commercial at the half of the football game.

"What does that even mean anymore?" I ask.
"Take all those kids," he says, "all those school shooters, all those terrorists. Same thing. Babies having tantrums, up here, you know?" He points to his head. "And here." He recoils his trigger finger. "If you're them, you're just looking for something you see all around & so want, but can't have." He grabs a handful of popcorn & continues:

"And yet, they don't even know how to handle it, even if one day they would get it. That's why a lot of them do suicide missions or shoot themselves in the head at the end."

The camera focuses high on the pigskin spiraling midair just after the kickoff.

"But this is really why they do it," he munches on. "You look all around, & deep down, you're damn afraid that the thing you most want to believe in this world doesn't even exist, maybe never did. Goodness, love, hope, truth. . . . *Unless* you can completely destroy it."

Above us, the Vikings fumble & Walid hoists his arms like he's already won our five-dollar bet.

BOX OF PERSONAL GODS

As a child I slept in a box of prayers,

Each night containing a slightly different problem sent far away like a
pathogen.

In another world they by now must constitute an entire otherly being, a
hideous creature

Surrounded by hinges and smashed lids, rusty and diseased.

One day I hope that monstrosity stomps back in search of me; demands

To know in which box I hoarded my purest laughter.

In which box I locked each unopened state of grace.

In which box ferment all those loveliest of human scents.

Of course, I expect, it will curse my extended hands; order me to go back
and revise every last label on my ancestors' good deeds and sins.

And when I am so old I can only sing sweetly at its menace, may that it foist
upon me a final, largest box

Full of mountains, trees, a river, and four horizons, then lay me down.

My dear, if only you'd paid attention, it will whisper, amid a kaleidoscope of
visions. *There is no immensity after this one.*

But I'll know: even the oldest box buried deep inside me has infinity between
each face.

PASSAGES

Ten thousand gods in the fields midblossom.
Overhead screeches a finned metal giant slithering
Its fast shadow over concrete straight through us like a bar-code scanner.

Illumined on a checkpoint screen, I watch a
Winged fetus in ultrasound. But it's only purple-
Striped socks, a hair dryer, six wallpaper samples.

Midmorning, daylight saving has a few confused.
Others smile or frown into the little black pools of their phones.
Palms and pink silk flowers along the moving concourse stand artificially
    at ease.

Midflight, dozing and dreaming, a pagan
Dance foregrounds a molten harvest moon
While evil trots a racehorse, combing its hair.

Antelopes plant plum trees with a hooked Bronze Age tool.
Come autumn, we won't ever arrive at the lighthouse.
Of course, we do finally scrape ashore. All winter

A dense figure on a trampoline flashes gang signs
By the village's bustling well. Near dead,
The fresh pulp of a far sawmill suddenly awakens my blind

Grandfather and four-year-old father,
Midforest, midblizzard. For a long time
After the plane lands and deboards

Nothing memorable happens.

ODE TO THE POEMS OF ANY SMALL NATION

*"For this reason poetry is more philosophical and more serious
than history ..."*
—ARISTOTLE, POETICS

On the other side of this heart
Runs a mountainous country.

Over that mountainous terrain
Scurries a speck of soul, unbounded—

My fourteenth great-grandfather, sneaking
Off to court a girl he has not been appointed by his father to marry.

By starlight, over streams and stones,
He approaches her cedar window.

See him: from shadows with nothing
Of his own to offer but a story

Of a typical day at school
On the other side of the mountain

Practicing calligraphy
And studying classical poems.

Would you want to hear one?
She is intrigued by his high, hoarse voice and plump earlobes.

I suppose.
He likes her jawline, her oil-black eyes by moonlight,

And the way her nose crinkles when she smiles at his
Nervous anecdotes.

They have no idea of the future
Already drawing together

Their adolescent limbs and organs
Amid cicadas in a cool breeze.

In less than two years, they will run off together.
With each passing season

Life will test them. She will die
In a fourth childbirth. He will lose an arm,

Thrown from a horse, then his right eye
On the eve of a colonial uprising.

Two of their children and several grandchildren
Will die over six decades in four wars. Their homeland to be

Divided by greed then need; starvation
Frozen inside the people's throats

Like all family stories never to be told.
But, for now, the young would-

Be scholar's ease grows, his elbows
On her windowsill, courting

This beautiful third daughter of the village miller,
Still both tentative with their eyes.

Nearby, a wooden wheel at the river grinds
Grain in time to his newest memorized poem

From the Koryŏ dynasty
Of two lone geese soaring through a mountain pass of purple irises

As barbarian soldiers fast approach.
Fifteen generations later, we know well the ancient ode

On his lips will stutter then stall in memory,
Requiring him to improvise something

Or appear foolish as if offering a broken gift.
As my eighty-nine-year-old aunt recounts:

My fourteenth great-grandmother's mind
Is already made up. She knows

This suitor and she are far too young.
She's not even that fond of poems,

Most of which seem to commemorate
Sadness, longing, loss.

Like the nearby water mill's insinuation,
The girl knows she wants a safe, steady life she can count on.

And then his eyelids fall.

ULTRASOUND

From nothing seem
to flicker our unborn
daughter's eyes

as one day mine will
power down. The transducer's
sonic resonances

on the screen not unlike
a photograph of my unborn
father's newlywed parents

decades before the war.
In a black suit and silk hanbok,
light pink or perhaps pale blue,

their adolescent faces float,
grainy as all unresolved fates.
There, at ten weeks

suddenly an image tumbles
across the monitor. An aftereffect
of loose-knit light

amid celestial dark
in this examination room
of only grains of light.

My love squeezes my hand,
swears she can already feel
a playful effervescence deep within.

Years before, in Anyang,
on the final evening visiting
that ninety-four-year old grandmother—

the only grandparent I have ever known—
I stooped to hug her good-bye,
her spine and shoulders

so frail and shriveled
I can still recall every curve and angle,
and her hand

gnarled like a seahorse
floating past dusk
from the window of my bus.

STILL LIFE WITH DUST WHILE LISTENING
TO AL JAZEERA NEWS OVER COFFEE

Geese gaggle & yawp across the horizon.

Late autumn, the last
Open window for months.

Meanwhile,
        Dust motes

Float past
        In the sunlight, spiraling

Small shaded bellies
Through our kitchen.
           Tiny paratroopers.

          Minuscule angels with clipped wings.

     Little spellbound humans, drowned

Millennia ago in a golden sea.

ABSCISSI●NS

SUPER-INSENSITIVE SPECIES

"Asian carp [introduced to control weeds and parasites] have been crowding out native fish, compromising water quality and killing off sensitive species."

—FROM "INVASION USA: ASIAN CARP INVADERS HAVE
TAKEN THE MISSISSIPPI, ARE THE GREAT LAKES NEXT?"
IN *SCIENTIFIC AMERICAN*

The Asian carp are on their way!
Thrumming waters, thrashing over dams midair.
You American engineers who released us

Into your streams and lakes, how could you forget
The Chinese Exclusion Act? Half-a-million
Topknots wishing not only to dig and blast but also breed?

I am young and shiny in Prada at the mall.
I am hunched at the bus stop, grease stained, smoky
Lungs full of sad erhu songs. Wok & Rolling

Through your suburbs, sardine-like in a Honda.
Hard down Wall Street on a Ducati rocket at 4 a.m.,
Paddle tennis rackets in my Gucci bag clattering.

A Bel Air clinic designed to disguise how to reenvision
This land of opportunity with even wider than Western eyes.
Koreatown Peaceful Cloud on Snake Mountain tattoos.

Myriad in late-night cram
Schools of swishing bubbles like slitty
Mermaids at your sailors' hulls.

Eating my own kind, even my own tail, to survive.
Feel our silvery fins sting through sludge and slime.
California and New York have long teemed with our disease.

Milwaukee and Chicago, how will your golden shores survive
Such frantic froth? From Olympia to Providence,
It's a new day, our forty-horsepower jaws so snappingly say, so

Bend over and drop your pants
Because the Asian carp are on their way!
Polishing your platinum ingots, boardroom doorknobs, and bylaws.

Maybe not yet the Whitest House, but fast
Scaling ourselves clean on the jagged edges
Of glass ceilings. Bottom dwelling

In deepest cyberspace. Chomping up bargain real estate.
How can the other fish possibly compete with no duck blood,
Biryani, pad thai, or kalbi sinew stuck between their teeth?

Melting pot, o.k. But not my fish head,
Not my GPA. Not my child's yellow
Lamborghini-shaped, Harvard-bound birthday cake. Reverse racism?

Affirmative action? Quota? What you say?
No no. We don't play that way.
Art of War jungle tunnels

Through your mind is our game.
And it's too late for you to learn
How to play. Because the Asian carp

Are on their way—dastaars bunched
Like three times the brain; shoguns blazing
Chopsticks and perfect SAT scores like rain.

Ancient saw-toothed devils shimmying up onto land
To squirm, crawl, stutter, walk about, and one day say:
Yo, where did all the Black

Elks, Standing Bears, and Pocahontases go?
Who rode off with all their horses, confiscating their guns?
Who over-forested then pumped green muck into rivers, thinning the salmon?

Whose sugar and cotton plantations enslaved?
Who converted whose heathen souls to fill whose churches and factories?
Who profited? Who outsourced?

Who instituted internment, the H1B visa, and the KKK?
Who bombed whose families' flesh and bones in Hiroshima, Korea, Vietnam,
    and Iraq
Back to the "Stone Age"?

Yes, the Asian carp are on their way
And life as it's known can't help but change.
But, really, if we must fish

For euphemisms—who
Brought whose eggs and minnows
Here to *invade* whose waters, land, and

Purity in the first place?

HIAWATHA HIGHWAY, MINNEAPOLIS

A ghost train just passed through me like a magician's saw
Bursting my favorite reveries into one
                                Endless reality. I didn't mind.
I could idle here forever in my car, straddling
These wrist-thin train tracks, decades defunct.
                       Before and after and beside me, other drivers
Wait for the traffic light that will mean we can inch and creep.
I spend more hours a week with them, and a cart-pushing Tibetan, and
    those three
Natives picnicking under the overpass with malt liquor and sunflower seeds,
Than I do with good friends.
            Sometimes when particularly gridlocked, there's time to step out
And root around through all the other limbs and severed incarnations
On the asphalt; all the years of office windows
Smeared horrifically right up against your sleep.
                        Eventually, though, the light
Turns to green enough times and the traffic
Herd rumbles forward into a world
No one has figured out yet how to love any better for more cash or a faster
    phone.
But it's there; you can smell it beneath the axle-grease heat of summer and
    drone of galvanized surf,
              Where once bison blinked patiently to cross back home.

PORTRAIT OF A BLIND COUPLE REVERBERATING

1.

You got light, asked the blind Slovak holding a Dublin pipe.
He didn't care his eyes might as well have been pecked by swallows and sun.
He was from Serbia, waiting for his wife to return from the mall.

Lifting my elbows off the dock rails, I offered to describe the scene for him:
white sails, waves, bundles of kelp.
A ponytailed crew team rowed through sunbeams.
                                        Once, a teenager had released a baby shark on a
dare, or so the locals told. The best catfish po'boy
was not in the overpriced pavilion, but a jerry-built shack behind the
     palm cove.

He was kind; let me talk, ramble on.
I was far from my life on a Tuesday afternoon.
My fiancée and job and dreams an impossible collage.
                                        In the end, the blind man reached
to rest his hand on my bare, sunburned shoulder
while intoning through a heavy accent, I think, about life not being a museum.
He was smiling. Maybe it was the sun.

2.

Each body is an ark. We store enough
clarity and obfuscation to survive. Stowaways be warned.
From the gathering dead that you will remember at least once a day until
     you die—immediate family, old friends, lovers—eventually all memories
coalesce and, as the Greeks depicted, soon
only brine and slippery seaweed surround.

3.

The old Slovak had slaved for decades in radio production: folk and classical
     music, then Communist Party public service announcements, then Fiat
     and Marlboro commercials after the Velvet Revolution.
Now retired, on his third honeymoon—after his high-school-sweetheart wife

left to open a garden shop in Tel Aviv; followed by a platinum-maned trophy
Pole who took the remainder of his investments when his sight ate itself.
But we always get by.
Eventually, the blind man's newest bride arrived, clicking planks with her cane.
Whiter haired than he; she was stooped in pink sneakers and carried a grin
of bemusement.
This my new friend, Edvard, he announced, and I took her soft, wavering hand.
The saltwater taffy and beef jerky she shared from the purchases for their
various grandchildren piqued my thirst. *The chocolate in your country
unsound,*
he translated for me after she giggled a snatch of Slovak to him.
Different, she corrected. *Sweet, very plain.* Cupping an expensive camera
with two hands, she asked: *You make please?*

They were a mess. Twist-mouthed and melted irises.
Bodies and oversized collars run over by the tractor of time.
Gorging on joy and madness, camped out alone together in a blank, windy
wilderness
buried impervious inside the sun.

I watched their pure delight disappear down the auburn shoreline long
until the ember of my own insignificance began to glow.

4.

Life is like photography. We develop from negatives. —Unknown

ON THE VELOCITY OF SOULS

Old souls tend
To gravitate toward ancient cities,
Dull coins, museums; wanting

To sense more waning power.
New souls tend to
Prefer bucolic landscapes:

Lakes, manageable woods, a suburb
With few reminders of the whole history of culture.
Sometimes it's reversed

And they'll cross paths, old and new souls,
Like a changing of the guards,
Even nodding along the road, trading news

Of ice ages, a rain
Forest turned desert, or
A particularly heinous human crime.

Plagues, jokes, undying
Lovers, genocides. On rare occasions
They'll even laugh, uncork a bottle

And share whatever sweet and salty
They have in their bags.
Because, ultimately,

Though always a little suspicious,
Old and new souls
Respect each other.

Unless one suddenly remembers
A judgment the other
Made eons ago

Instead of translating the poem.

HALOS

Blood vessels are invading
both corneas, crowding
the sclera, says my ophthalmologist.

Not an emergency yet, but
just be aware and get proper rest. I ask
about laser surgery and he sighs; confesses

when his own eyes are shot, he'll
surgically insert acrylic lenses.
Two slits, no stitches, fifteen minutes.

With lasers, you'd still need
readers and eye drops. On my walk
home, I take off

my glasses to receive the breeze.
I like that any nearing face
is surely smiling, gorgeous;

each blurry body's aura numinous:
style of no style, racially
ambiguous, a glob, pure

spectral incohesion. Aren't we all
just masses of energy and light
approaching or leaving

one another in the jumbled
future or past; sometimes stop-
ping to embrace

for a moment or decades,
before passing
way too far for sight?

That visual impairment improves hearing,
taste, smell, touch is mostly myth.
With it, however, I can detect

fuzzy spirits exiting buildings;
halos around bikers' helmets;
each streetlamp another pink-orange dawn.

You should see the full moon
spanning half the skyline.
I don't mind opening a book

like a pewter Rorschach test,
or waking up each morning
inside a fish tank of dream.

I like, whenever I wish, strolling past
the myopic me
in a window or mirror or whatever

reflects back to believe the soul is
ubiquitous like water
in our voices, our cells.

How else, when blinded by life,
would I remember:
to the dead, we're the ghosts?

CENTRIFUGE

Before passing on   or beyond   or through

my uncle hypothesized that the Large Hadron Collider in Switzerland
     could in reality be a time machine thirteen governments were covertly
     collaborating on, ostensibly to confirm the existence of the Higgs boson
     or "God particle."

We went around & around his dinner table, but never did
convince the other's   synapses   alimentary   pathways
          epigenetic
                    streams   of   the
                                        validity   of   the

other's perceptions
                    of   reality,   whipping
          sloshing   scintillating
          around & around   in each   separate   blood
                                             bone
               chromosomal
                                                  ghost
                                                       container.

Older now, I get the nonliteral point of this former captain in the ROK
     (Republic of Korea) Army, who later earned a PhD in physics at
     Stanford, before whirling on to hold numerous patents in aeronautical
     engineering:

               I want the world to be safe, but am experiencing a crisis of faith
amid all its
mounting   technology   &   weaponry   like the head   of a pin
& a trillion blind-
folded
                    angels   fossilized
                              in Bình Hòa.

46

It was a cool Sunday evening in their dining room in Northern California.

We ate incomprehensibly sweet nectarines & *gimbap & lychee & cuttlefish*
    from a wooden bowl *on a blanket along the Han River,*
            Come on in it's warm, my uncle, still trim, with all his black
      wavy hair, kept   splashing
                    & calling   *to the rest of*
         us on shore,   *everyone   laughing—*

Then I drove back to my dormitory, contemplating every particle & wave
    in every possible form
               (in)significant
            as one
                      hot summer   evening's
                        sweet fishcake-on-a-stick
                      at a cinema ganged with
bodies in Myeong-dong   where projected onto the screen was a remake of
    some myth in the form of a medieval scientist who keeps
        trying to widen a
        portal he's created to bring back
        his daughter killed in an imperial canon blast.
            Each time
        the madman readjusts his bamboo dial for the cerulean-lit wormhole,
        a slightly new & arbitrary set of memories fills each character
        without any of their lives knowing it.

GWANGJU

They were lost   In a country where everything screams green cab
and the only water—dream-tongue   slow and oceanic spittle
The father's face interrogated   into a street sign
The mother's way   with plants all feasted upon by soldiers
ganged into rusted thought trains The sister was
there, but selling faceless clocks an aquarium on a corner
Everyone else was a cousin   never met
You were there too   asking directions for
                    a bayonet
                                  Everywhere—natives with hot black sails
for hair   So you forced,
                    peeled away a face
to reveal the sky's cords
                    all more vocal than your own

None reasonable nor lovely enough to swallow   And once again, you were mistaken
answering the wrong question

But the horse-faced streetwalker wouldn't let go   What you remember now:
Her smoky, torn voice   her bandaged hand guiding
past children cheering a helicopter's military loud a story of a nearby shack on a
                                                    mountain
speaker
                    farmed into a grain of sand

Nothing of the hills' burned-down Buddhist temples   the looted tombs at the hem of

                    her sun-scored cheekbone

The land's yellow loess whispered   *You could go deeper*
and   *Beware the rutting*
American dump trucks—small and distant   enough to churn any old thought
song
                I take you each evening to the clouds,
                                  howled her pimp, hobbling

This, a languid traveler's further logic:

Maybe he was instead a ghost
in
all the skyscrapers, karaoke bars, banks,

and she loved him
another time before
U.S. Army red-light camp towns

If you saw both of them cajoling,
you too may have hoped for

tugging at one of my sleeves
a disgorgement of silver and

peonies—

In whichever lifetime,

At whichever dusk

your own tide bleeds

ALIEN FAITHS

when young   i was sure   we were   being

farmed   from afar   not

for our bodies   or labor   but our capacity

to love

which the aliens   lacked

as now humans   cultivate

algae

to absolve   our toxic   waste

our   oil

spills—

later   i was   certain

it's not our   love   but

our
faith

in a higher   order   or purpose

or god

the aliens required

to survive   as we do
oxygen

from plants—

i now

understand

all

the concern   and   longing

inside

my body   will   one day   be

                              no more

than a rutabaga   to its once-   seed's   hull—

                                                                                no
                                                                                more

than a family's   excess   flowers
                        left behind   at a
              funeral

home—

              which is to say   those flowers'
         faith

in   whatever   we are

                        able   to perpetuate
                        through

         our   bodies   our   thoughts

of loveliness
                        and decay—

                                              the   greater   those
                                        flowers'
faith   the   more   blessings

         for the living   left   beside

the dead
in all their

                        alien

                                                        grace

A SUPERIMPOSITION

"Do not go back to sleep . . ."
                    —RUMI

Tonight, the boxcars beyond this office window hiss; flaunt
their graffiti, plotless,
                    trundling
celluloid frames of rust at dusk—

You glance up
                    at passing creosote, hickory, and coal;
the climate control always too cold or warm;
if somebody gets sick, half in the office start sniffling
until mutations ransack.

Once, while alone, you saw him:
                    a gray-haired hobo rumbling past,
stretching his long arms in a Northern Pacific boxcar
meant for shingle-grit sand or feed corn,
                    and ever since
        have been leery of his return.

A smoky man, gaunt in a slicker of trash bags, blinking at the coming night.

Next time, ignore him.
Do not rise to switch off the lights
or lift your hand to the glass.
                    He is no one:
a singed being in the autumn afterlight, an ember
winking in his lips; jettisoning
snot with one index finger like a button, across azure waves of prairie grass
    and milkweed.

He has no interest in you or your cubicle; steel-
alloy thoughts too rhythmic; synaptic clanks
already far away in other states,
                    towns, fields, mountains, valleys—

Whoever he was, wherever he is now,
he couldn't care less about some hologram
in a collar and a twenty-two-dollar noose,
                              ablaze in yet another office's passing
fluorescence like lightning inside its aquarium.
He wants only what he can kill, or will do the same to him.

A REAL MAN

I had a therapist who volunteered that his father
once reached for and covered his schoolboy eyes, turning
his little head away from a white-linen funeral procession passing in front
    of their house in Taiwan.

Years later, I remember nothing else
about our conversations over those several months, but that, and the end.

We'd clearly reached an impasse in his basement
office—an old and a young man, mirroring the other's tension.

I like to think I at least said good luck upon our final meeting.
But he'd returned to his desk and was already writing in his tea-
and suncake-stained notebook, his hand quivering oddly.

It was dark, midwinter. Inside my car
I stared and stared, only half aware
of the highway, the slanting snow,

half recalling the night a doe fractured its spine
against our Dodge's front grille and windshield,
and my father made me fetch him the tire iron.

GOSSIP

Humans lacked humility by fearing death, so the gods created books and endowed them with stories and living skin, commanding the people to build elaborate libraries instead of elaborate cemeteries.

Most obediently complied. In time, however, some grew inspired to revise, until the stories and books became more alive than most humans.

For the first time ever the gods grew annoyed. The strongest stories could no longer be contained in books—or humans. Certain of the characters had already begun to speak righteously, indignantly, fearlessly of a world in which even a god must be humbled more and more, revision after revision, until no longer distinguishable from an atom.

TEARS OF TEARS

I cried so hard I began to laugh. Or the reverse. Regardless,

I'd inadvertently created yet another universe. First, I felt shame

for losing control of my body and mind. Amid increasingly painful guffaws,

I glimpsed my teeth midair and no longer knew my name. I'd

always had a slight accent in the language of tears, which I was self-

conscious about, but now in the language of laughter I was completely fluent.

Suddenly, babies started flowing out of my pores. I couldn't stop

them from leaving this world to become gods in the next. Eons passed,

until my laughter began to subside and the last child to flow

up and out of my belly button said: *Man, you can come with us if you want.*

I thought about it, then declined. Said: *If I go now, I may not remember*

my pain, and on that pain is written a long list of things I want

to remember when I'm dead. Said: *I better stop all this nonsense and get*

back to the serious business of decorating the expansive caverns deepest

inside my loneliness. Off the last teardrop went from my body, howling,

quivering, shaking its head at what I'd just said, higher and higher into a vast

ocean of crenulated sky, until the sun once again began to shine.

CAN

The aluminum soda can rattled along in the wind, in search of others with a similar tone.

Lonely and sun-faded, it had gotten separated from its pack days before.

But the sadistic wind kept trying to introduce the can to common trash—old magazines, a soiled tampon, wet leaves.

After some weeks, the can broke free from a highway underpass in a late-spring torrent.

Now it was no longer so flimsy and naive. Now its belly contained something of what it had seen of the wild winds of change, and so rolled with a new authoritative volition.

Eventually, an old man, a can pimp with filthy fingers, picked it up, and crushed it to the size of a hockey puck under his boot heel.

Tossing it into a plastic bag filled with a hundred other demoralized cans, the can pimp went along his way.

Meanwhile, the bagged cans kept crying for help in their own crushed-can tongues; their bellies, fermenting with rain, sugar, sand, yeast, and maggots, had already gotten a taste of freedom, and they did not want to be reprocessed back into good, clean, uniformly smooth objects of function.

The opposite of Santa Claus in every way except for his beard, the can pimp pedaled his rusty bicycle, whistling obliviously despite the clamoring load of cries and pleas slung over his shoulder.

Meanwhile, in the jerry-built cart behind his bicycle, a second clear garbage bag of glass bottles clinked and chimed a very different tune, refusing to cry or gnash discordantly about like their metal counterparts every time the can pimp encountered a pothole.

At one point, as the sun was setting, the can pimp swerved and teetered to one side on his bicycle, first against a parked car, then hard onto the asphalt. Instantaneously, the hundred-plus crushed cans tumbled out, spilling over the road to buffer his fall. Even on their death march, they could not help but be cheap and useful.

The three dozen or so clear glass bottles responded very differently. Upon impact with the asphalt, they too somehow joyously broke free, clinking and chiming in all directions to celebrate their newfound freedom.

However, their jubilation was premature. The can pimp, shaken but uninjured, simply rose, mumbling to himself, and methodically went about re-collecting every last container—glass or metal—strewn across the road, never mind the honking cars . . .

All but a single crushed can, that is, which somehow slipped through the metal bars of a storm drain—down to where, to this day, it remains, deeply wary of any semblance of potential redemption.

PUPA HEART

                    The
         homeless   man
         resting   against
            the   downtown bank,   coughing   &
        laughing to himself,   is not so   different from
        the   chrysalis   scraping
                              & flickering   in its   paper-
        thin shell.
                    He's becoming   a god.   The pupa
        will soon be a butterfly.
                         The human   inside   you might
        offer   some   coffee,   a bill,
                                   or some   change.
        When   the   big   bang   scattered   its news,
                    dark   energy   in   the   garden
        bloomed   so   aroused   its pods
        clustered   into   stars.
                                   I'm not speaking
        of forever,   more   joyful   fruit   in   the   afterlife.
        Spiders,   parasitic   flies,   wasps   hector
            butterflies
                         all summer.   Infinite demons   & angels
        decorate theater sets inside   any soul.   I'm   saying:
        the next time   you   observe,
            that   homeless   man's   oil
            stain   on   old   cardboard,   or   the
                opaque
                cocoon,   once   dangling
                from   your   mailbox,
                                   is now   torn
                    wide open—
                              take care,
            your heart   burns
                enough   hunger
                &   grace   before   it   too
                gnaws   through   the
                    fabric   of   time,
                              astonishing

                    faith.

PASSENGERS

A stoic, white-haired couple in our favorite café glances up
Over their path-worn chessboard
To smile at one another and inter-
Lock fingers—the Kinks

On vinyl through wireless speakers, enjoining their eyes.
Like two tortoises recalling a typhoon
Once ridden to a far, spuming coast;
Delight in each other's leathered flesh, long carved.

Strolling home, you and I pass two ducks splashing down into a pond.
A drunk couple helps each other off the bus.
Sudden fire sirens. A distant Amtrak.
Wind pantomiming the receipt-tongue of a plastic bag.

Once, in bed, you mumbled, *Where did I come from, how did I find you?*
Decades or days before or later, in a dream
I whispered your name at the dice in my fist—
The stakes life and death—
                              and rolled
Red and yellow leaves through a breezeway.

IN THE KEY OF IRON WIND CHIMES

Every morning, the iron wind chimes beyond our open window clang

A different tune depending on the wind's mood. Today a silvery
tintinnabulation

About washing a minor god's ivory-thread hair, blustering at the edge
of a waterfall.

Old and confused, she believes it's winter and so keeps trying to climb
the long-

Thawed streams and diaphanous globs, splattering against algae-skinned
stones.

In reality, it's the height of summer. The attendants simply chuckle,
feed, then tuck

The old muttering deity into her usual bed of leaves and fallen branches—

Come autumn, the few most pious attendants hold themselves alone,
wondering

Where that minor god went, and if she will ever return to keep her
wild promises to all the butterflies and trilliums and moths in some
distant garden.

In deep black, the idle attendants, begin to gossip—a descending hush:

*Maybe that old deity was an imposter, and that's why her songs never possessed
any discernible construction.*

What if nothing about her drove those miraculous seasons?

*And of all the gold and platinum promised to tower through our bones to heaven—
what if they were only bars she'd briefly escaped like a child from its pen,
or lunatic?*

What then—of our landscape, its depiction?

Eventually, even those final two attendants must go—and we rise, yawning
to the sun's newest refrain.

COLONIZING A
DIFFERENT SUN

MITOCHONDRIAL EVENING

"One tiny piece of our DNA *is inherited only down the female line. . . .*
Some molecular biologists say that, aeons ago, the mitochondrion
was a free-living organism with its own DNA, *and possessed the*
secret of generating lots of energy."
    —"MITOCHONDRIAL DNA: THE EVE GENE" BY STEPHEN
    OPPENHEIMER

There is a woman and a man
naked inside me, though
they have yet to properly meet.
This began long ago, before
time. Before memory
or art, when even cave
walls awaited nostalgia
in one spectral cell.
The woman and man
morphed over millennia, trading
notochords and ectoderms,
but this remained constant: he loved
when the woman sang in joy,
in sadness; he loved
that he, the man, could not
enter into her voice without
leaving behind all
he knew how to savage
for their children. Eventually,
he fashioned a tail to better
find her, and she more sensitive
filaments and corona. His
greatest gift, the shoulder
he built to hurl slings. Soon
together they willed the best vista
from the height of a mountain.
Grottos filled with skulls.
Meanwhile, he honed consonants;
she polished her vowels. Time

came and iron separated
safety from chaos. Still their children escaped
through the days and hours.
Still the woman and man sometimes
traded turns stomping off
into darkness. Fierce
declarations. She within the man inside her
daughters and sons could only
listen to him paint
disturbing glyphs of his mother's
dreams. This man, you see,
despite sharpened tools
did not yet understand that no
document is imperishable;
that any immutable covenant
has no name. The woman
suffocating in her own father's nightmares
termed this faith. The man drowning in the
woman's pain cursed anyone fearful.
Their children tearfully prayed. Sometimes
I hear them, my man and woman,
arguing, or making love,
it's not always clear. One
woman inside me, my great-
grandmother, whispers
to her lover on a straw mat
that one day they will escape
to a beautiful country where
people can marry whomever they wish.
The one atop the other smiles, wonders
what it would be like far beyond
this family's rice fields. Giggling
in the cellar of a pavilion, breaths
like fragrant soup, they kiss
then oversleep.
                        Far away, one distant
ancestor inside my grandmother
is at war, fleeing

communists, barbarians, giant
hyenas, drones. Every decision
he makes will determine 8 percent
of the planet's chromosomes.
One daughter within him will love the lute so
melancholy my piano keys tinge blue.
In a world ruled by women, the saying goes,
there would be no war. At least one
mean girl inside me is skeptical.
The old man selling arrows and seeds
deep in my spine has no comment.
Everyone within his daughter's wavy hair
murmurs: it all depends
on the kind of love inherited
from one's parents.
                              Where
does any mother end and a father begin
if all marriages not a century back
meant entitlement to her ovaries? For eons
the women inside me have taught
their most prideful brothers how to let go.
For eons the men inside me have
shown only how to burn and rebuild.
Where now, in which direction? asks
one to the other, lost in a forest
fairy tale that slithers like syntax
confused. Both think they know,
but lately withhold their sweetest apples.
                              In moonlight, a female
shadow is touching itself. No. The male
within her is reshaping his fate
by her fingers and palm.
Have you ever heard a woman
bayoneting a bear? A man weep
in a maternity ward? The mustache-
and-lingerie-wearing sphinx
inside both of us thinks women
are always cock-blocking the apocalypse.

She straps on a cattle prod
and chuckles with her fellow
guards holding cameras and phones. The whore
moaning in a mask on bloody cement
unsheathes his hidden janbiya,
readies the blade. Odds
are someone has raped
multiple bodies still cowering
in your DNA. Odds are some distant outlier in your
progeny will maim or kill.
Bodies will burn and a few
saints in you will eventually
save millions of souls. If only
we could reframe the myth
of innocence and whores; the myth
that there can be no peace without war.
Of course, the me in we loves
to ennoble myself. Loves to believe
the human spirit always grows
in the direction of an angel's flashlight.
Yet the sage inside every child knows
in searching for the other, the man
inside the woman inside the animal, you find
distorted truths, which frighten
everything but the soul.
                              Still
the male enshrined in me is reluctant
to traverse to his most she-wolf self. Several women
in him are waiting for their sons
to finally grow some teeth and move
out of the basement. No. She can't
ponder a thing, is too busy walking past
a broken streetlamp. Meanwhile,
the man in my body watches through curtains
a new, larger army, and questions
what all the girls will think if he doesn't volunteer.
No. He's listening
to his sisters already in uniform curse

the end of races and God as a machine
pumps their milk.
                    There
is a woman and a man naked inside me
who have yet to fully uncleave.
This was long ago, before moon
and sun. Both reincarnated a wild
bestiary of beings over eons,
but this remained constant:
the woman loved when all
the fathers inside all their grandmothers inside all
their grandchildren harmonized in a song
of sadness, joy, tribulations; loved
when each time, without fail,
two lovers danced to their respective border's edge
and waited, with their books and musical instruments,
breathing softly into each other
all their most secret sins.
                    Meanwhile, the old ones
convinced all the guards
to dream of a myth that would shed the earth's heaviest robes.
And to long for every girl in your laughter was to fly.
And to fly was to rediscover each boy
buried alive.
                    There is a language
within the man I am—dying
at different speeds, the language
an ocean, the human a sea whose
tributaries like frost on a window or vines
on a wall only sometimes in places cross.
I'm looking at one right now
as the child I used to be. Or
are they the veins in my mother's
womb. Or diffuse red
emissions from a cosmos too far away
to revise anything on this evening
but my father's burial clothes.

ELECTRICAL STORM

Light kisses and imprints itself upon our cells
as culture records the past and future
on sheet after sheet of sleep.

In one recurring dream, we are late for a ballet,
shadowed under a boiling moon across icebergs.
In another, our black walnut tree keeps bombardiering

its little brains out, trying to split the heavens wide open.
All liquid remembers where it came from, thus is song.
You were sad that rainy evening, so I drank

happiness enough for us both. Our love
is sometimes like a large pond with only two ducks.
I remember opening you

into words, gently, with a single question.
You were a vision and I the lightning.
Wind, thrashing

hurricane. All desire
locked in the body's ancient water is sweet,
I believe. As it's never what a lover says, but the melody.

To listen to any rain is the history of love
in love with thick, wild grain. Even
when the thunderstorm keeps changing its tune.

Cymbals, drums. A half-ton
branch lands in a far street of four a.m. car alarm
symphonies. In darkness,

at a border that defines two
dreams, someone
mumbles another's name, falling

into a pair of stiff, crushed
wings long and far into morning.

POSTELECTION POEM, NOVEMBER

I was wrestling with a poem
while in a far room she was crying.
I'd been sweating to get it to sing
or speak eloquently, at least exorcize the animus from our deeply lodged insanity.

Meanwhile, in her far room, Babygirl would not go back down.

I needed personally to hear through the poem
what future humans will believe in the next few millennia
of horror, tenderness, genocide, altruism, capacity for deceit, of beauty—

I didn't understand that she was already openly translating,
while the poem I hunched over lay comatose.

Our policy: wait five to ten minutes before going in.
Often, after a final, hawk-like screech, she'd fall quiet, until I could breathe again.
But on this night, the longer she wailed, the more deaths shed from me,
until finally at the risk of waking her forever
I rose and walked into the dark corner of our galaxy
where a deeper belief in the brightness of human souls
was now livid in its demand for a new kind of poetry.

PATHOLOGY OF HAPPINESS

Happy people don't have to understand other people. Some call this total
   freedom.
To others it's ignorance, edging into sin—the source of all society's woes.

But happy people don't need to listen to anyone. *I am my own planet in a
   solar system*
*of neighboring planets similar enough to mine, all circling a divine sun. Perhaps
   farther planets circle many more suns, but such mysterious things beyond
   my control are no real concern of me and mine.*

And for a time all goes relatively well. Until war, once again, arises between
   the happy and the unhappy people. The former try to convince the happy
   people that they are not truly happy, only ignorant, selfish, indifferent.
   But the happy people, far less conflicted and stressed, usually win. Unless
   they allow themselves to become tainted and believe maybe they aren't
   so happy, maybe they've been living a lie their whole lives at the expense
   of others less happy than them.

Typically, then, only two options remain: to become deeply sad, or happier
   than you've ever been!

FRAGMENT OF CIV—

[. . .] until a sickness moved in and hung over the city like a long absence of wind. Soon, people simply stopped speaking their truest feelings. Late at night, some researched its origins. Space aliens, clandestine military experiments, chemicals in the water. But their findings only inoculated them from polite conversation. Meanwhile, a subsequent generation of the sickness was already making certain susceptible people speak of their feelings all the time. Some understood the ridiculousness of this, yet couldn't help themselves. *It's the sickness,* they thought, which made them feel better. Like a longest winter, the sickness settled in, making people create all kinds of distractions from its grip on their lives: new inventions, relationships, businesses, books, economies, art, regimes, interpretations. But these were all only diversions from the knowledge that the sickness now defined them; that it was no longer a sickness but the norm. In fact, both faux pas and public laws discouraged behavior to the contrary. Animals and creatures who'd managed to avoid the sickness retreated farther away and into themselves. Most of their unsick kind died alone. Some people blamed humanity for threatening to destroy the planet. However, they too were sick and so couldn't fully articulate the deeper truth—that, by now, the sickness within people and also their pets was as comfortable as flowers and weeds thriving in a landfill. It's unclear what happened next. Human beings more or less disappeared, and the sickness, for a long, ambiguous period, fell dormant. Until the few creatures that remained finally recognized that the sickness they'd been born into was not a nuisance like boils or mold but a gift from a long time ago that was to be cherished as a kind of first fire. Inspired by this, they built monuments in praise and worship of the sickness they now believed had saved only them. Life continued on like this for many years, until, one spring, a stronger sickness arrived that immediately everyone recognized and feared for the vague premonitions, and sense of shame they now felt for the lives they had been living.

COLONIZING A DIFFERENT SUN

1.

"It's easy to love when you haven't lost everything," my mother would never say.

Instead: "I don't need to text."

"We think we're not sliding into evil like a ship over the horizon to those on deck," she's only intimated.

But, very clearly, this: "Take your daughter to church in a language she doesn't understand; let her *feel* the others singing, then let her decide for herself."

And this one, though not to me, and not in English: "When your heart is broken in two, that's when you must gently hold yourself into a new layer of truth."

Once, while watching TV, she explained (I translate): "North and South Korea are like lobes of the brain. Both will fall into mistrust of one another for periods, then reconcile, then fight again. It has to do with a longer history than anyone understands. Like running requires a fleeting moment of disequilibrium, then a burst of faith, and so on. You can cover much more ground this way than walking."

"Ideology is a flag with stolen, fraying wings and garish colors sewn on," she whispers, after a sip of barley tea (for her eyesight). "Hope is only truly useful when it's deeply buried blue."

And finally this from my mother's mouth: "Civil war is a fever that either kills the infection or the host. Look at the rich and poor here now, everywhere. You know, I was reading of an American soldier, a Puerto Rican, who defected to Russia in the sixties, where he still lives with his family and enjoys fishing and painting outside of Moscow. The most interesting part of this machinist's account" (I translate her words from the man's Spanish-accented, broken Russian as aired on the Seoul-based news show's translation into Korean that she'd watched):

Everything we say is a series of inverse sonic waves.
Yet people forget collectively their voice is stronger than an atomic bomb.
If everyone shouted their demands at the same time, the world could
    electromagnetically change.
If everyone in just one country whispered all at once it could clean and transform
    the ethical landscape.
When you make art and songs and poetry you change your own and others' atoms.
Yet so few people think they really can.
The outward manifestation of this collective frustration and friction then
    becomes the making of more and more bombs.
All so one day we can all be brought to our knees, our skin peeling off, our souls
    like earthworms after a long rain . . .

2.

The dream kept rousing me, but too gingerly.
Miles and miles of factories and people standing at conveyor belts
Like oyster shuckers, polishing little metal replica national flag pins
    with tiny brushes and a gummy gray cream—

Thousands of women and men, examining thousands of different national
    flag pins,
None of which I recognized, none of which any of the hair-netted workers wore
    on their own blue smock lapels.

Meanwhile, to the west, several suns, like peaches of various sizes and stages
    of ripe, hovered above or partially tucked behind a mountain range.

I was wearing some regime's official gray uniform. As I was leaving
Someone placed their gloved hand (blue latex) on my right shoulder's
    epaulet, and said:

Comrade, don't be afraid. Everyone here holds your same human
Fate, shimmering
Like a coin in a shallow brook.

(He too was fluent in dreamspeak.)

When I turned around, I saw the dude who repairs and collects money
    from the vending machines at work, Mugbil, who, when I'm stressed, I
    sometimes bum Camels from.
Under his thin blue smock, he wore a "Free Mumia" t-shirt.
Still gripping my shoulder, he smiled, and asked if I wouldn't mind taking
    one of the national replica pins back to his family in Mogadishu.
o.k., I said.
He smacked his pack of menthols and flicked one up like a magician.
The pin had North Korea's newest Great Leader's face engraved on it. I
    pressed it against my forearm, to see if the likeness would appear, but it
    only partly did.

Everything is a social construction, Mugbil exhaled. He raised a hand to
   indicate the bustling operation behind us. *Power is the only real factory.*
He exhaled another light-blue cloud of smoke in which I could make out
   a few dozen ideograms, then continued: *It's all theater. North Korea is
   only the latest political reality show. They all are. Attila. Every pope. Khan.
   The European kings and queens. Mussolini. Hitler. Chavez. Saddam.
   Berlusconi. The Founding Fathers, and every American president. So don't
   get your hopes up.*

Now we were walking, and eventually he led me out into a garden.

*My forefathers arrived from Egypt and settled on the coast of Somalia in 1875.
   The French and Anglos followed. Italy with their spaghetti after that.
   Britain. Socialism. Clan warfare. Divide and conquer. U.S. U.N. al–Shabab.
   Pirates. Kenya. African Union. American drones. And we aren't even yet
   out of act 1.*

The garden, you could tell, was listening.

I remembered hearing from an arborist once that he always visited a tree
   a few times before amputating a limb so that the tree could become
   familiar with him. He did it, he claimed, so that it and the other trees
   around would be prepared to mourn. And also so they wouldn't invoke
   a chemical hex, as he put it, to bring retribution and sadness upon him.

This gave me sympathy for the grim reaper.

You still have family in North Korea? Mugbil took a seat on a bench under a
   great white birch.
I nodded.
*My family in Somalia is really into both K-pop and the ongoing North Korea
   drama,* he continued. *Venezuela's Lifestyles of the Corrupt and Damned
   is up and coming, though. And yet, something about that show already feels
   like a rerun. You think your mother knows anyone who could get the Great
   Leader's autograph?*

From a minaret to the west, a call to prayer issued, in the opposite direction
     of the national replica pin-making plant. Mugbil rose, as if he'd been
     waiting for this adhan his entire life.

I have something else for you, he said.
He unrolled his prayer rug and handed me an old-school answering
     machine, then rattled a box of minicassette tapes in a box.
Think twice about listening, though, he said.
I put my finger on "play," but he placed his cool, dry hand over mine.
Birch leaves spiraled down all around.
Suddenly, the majestic white hairs in his eyelashes made him look tired.
O.K., he said. O.K. *But I did warn you.*
He then took the answering machine's cord and squished the prong
     through a wound in his skull.

3. INDIAN GIVER

The New World wanted to open poems for all eternity—
Gifts from God, each one a cell, a molecule,
Quarks and neutrinos, etcetera—
                              It doesn't matter
The fashionable wrapping paper.
Billions, trillions
Of them every second passing through your thumbnail.

And inside each resplendent new discovery, more gifts!
Certain gifts were meant to be enjoyed and shared.
Others to be in awe of, revered.
Hence, crimes against humanity arose.

So God conjured one final gift,
Burying it deep within everything, everyone,
And wrapped it in a solemn promise

To forever distort Itself.

4.

I remember hating my voice on answering machines before we all entered
     the digital wormhole.
My voice recorded here, now, as zeros and ones, I don't mind at all; its vocal
     shadowlessness, clearly not able to record the soul.

Recently, before my mother's answering machine disappeared for good, I
     listened
to it in her living room, where for years it had sat like a safety lockbox.
No one else was home for Christmas.
I listened to an old message I'd left almost two decades earlier
Hello? Hello? Is anyone there? (click)
And also: *Hey just calling to say happy birthday . . .*
And also: *Dad, we got done early, can you pick me up?*

Because all those voices were so different than the one I currently had,
I was pleasantly surprised to find something pleasing about them, like
     someone I'd like
to get a beer or have a glass of chocolate milk with.

So I called the answering machine from my cell phone and left a message.

The words I uttered, however, were not the ones I heard being left on the
     answering machine. Instead, my mouth from this digital wormhole
     said: *Testing, testing, one two three,* as any technician checking
     communication equipment floating in space.

Listen, I don't have much time.
The world has changed in ways you can't possibly imagine.
There are no more countries.
No more planets. I haven't spoken any human language like this in years.
     Sorry if I'm rusty.
There are no words you'll understand for the way we live now.
There was an explosion.

Now I could hear the garage door opening and see my mother's car pulling
   up on the driveway.
The voice on the analogue answering machine also went quiet.

Carefully, I spoke again into my cell phone:
I don't want whatever information you're peddling . . .

As I spoke, so too did my/the voice being recorded:

I am the reason you were born.
I am the reason Mom and Dad were born.
I am the reason our grandparents, and their parents, were born, ad infinitum.
Yet, I'm you, thoroughly you.
Just not any you you know.
You can't see me through all the iron bars of ideologies . . . postmodernism . . .
   the aftereffect of religion, of books and films . . .

The garage door was closing.

I thought:
But I finally like me exactly the way I am.

What you believe to be your country will burn.
There will be nowhere in four dimensions to go.
Pure energy is every possibility all at once.
Conviction is all there is at the center of every atom.
Karma is more real than gravity.
It utilizes it as humans do language.
You won't understand anything more.
I need to send you an interpreter.
Do you want a son or daughter?

5. *"If I feel physically as if the top of my head were taken off, I know that is poetry."* —Emily Dickinson

Before passing on, my father, who never got to read anything I'd written, recounted the decapitation of a teacher in a cornfield over half a century earlier. They'd been forbidden to speak Korean in their own land, by the Japanese who had to that point colonized the peninsula for twenty-seven years. All native children got assigned a Japanese name on their first day of school. Japanese grammar pamphlets were handed out to study for eventual matriculation into a nearby middle school, over which a pair of imperial flags flew like dragon-red eyeballs. The baker's son had eczema, a chubby face, and lived in my father's neighborhood in Seoul. This boy bragged of sleeping with his Japanese grammar book under his pillow. Even when playing stickball in an abandoned munitions dump with friends, he refused to speak or even shout or fight in his native tongue. The way my father described it, the boy wanted badly to be Japanese and win a scholarship to university in Tokyo. One day the baker's son reported their Korean math teacher to the Japanese headmaster for reciting a classic Korean poem after lunch on a grassy hill. Their math teacher was a learned man, a poet, but not one of the dissidents or spies that had been sabotaging Japanese government trucks and other vehicles. Thickly bespectacled, this wiry Korean with a reedy voice spoke fluent Japanese and German, loved Wordsworth, Goethe, Schopenhauer, Lermontov, Kim Sowol. My father couldn't remember the title of the poem their math teacher recited in their native tongue on that windy afternoon surrounded by tall grass. *But very moving,* he recollected. *Our teacher closed his eyes, like this, and to our small, knowing ears, a beautiful, horrific opera flowed as if watching crows.*

6. TO THOSE IN CHILDHOOD WHO ONCE DREW A CORNFLOWER BLUE COFFIN THAT WAS SECRETLY A SPACESHIP TO BYPASS HEAVEN

welcome

your old memories already

contain all future storage

facilities beyond your brain

WHY

The castle where I happened upon the roundness of suns

Was an island prison on the ocean

No one visited my distractions here

Or my joys or sins

A sanctuary of sound and sense

The waves brought creatures and seaweed I could eat

The trees provided palm honey

Hot wind in leaves fanned me to sleep

I was happy

Eventually all the memories inside me congealed

Like the songs of jellyfish soaring through tides at dusk

Sometimes I confused myself for pure desire

Sometimes I only closed my eyes, and returned

To that border where wisdom and beauty debated all night

In a tavern populated by the sad parents of artists and politicians

But always reality, in some garden, replanted my name

Always a cool rain eventually reanimated my face

After decades, near blind from sun, I built a giant driftwood dollhouse

Gave the figurines octopus hearts and star fruit hair

Whales serenaded my presence along the shoreline

Birds offered news of the world

Though I had no interest in honing my beliefs or assumptions into
    stick-thin weapons

An endless chain of old friends, the seasons

Infrequently visited in gentle reminiscence of one another's passing

And when death finally drowned the last song in my lungs with stars

On rare evenings I too could glance down

Past corrugated carpets of pink-lit clouds—far

To that island castle on the sea where every day

I was free to genuinely miss me

THEY MET IN A SONG

They met in a song. Or, the song realized its fullest self inside them. They married and had a child who sang. Where did her song come from?

Her song was testing itself; could not yet fly, could not yet create a song that spawned new songs, but it could bring a smile to strangers' faces at the grocery store.

Where does any song come from? The singers know while singing. The writers know while listening. The instruments know precisely where each unearthed song aches: in tree trunks, raw ore, veins threading deep through the earth—as if in search of tunes to release their exquisite caresses against fingers and lips.

Some songs live longer in recordings, on paper, in bones. When all those are destroyed, all listeners gone, will the songs return where they came from, or reblossom?

Until then, each song is listening how to grow fuller. A human being's hands have only begun to dream across the keys. But the song is always there. A cosmos of notes amid darkness, suddenly free as tears of laughter.

Bodies shining with sweat like searchlights.
Lips tiptoeing secretly along.
Soles shaping swaying souls.

I don't know how many other lives have been saved by a song. I don't know how many soldiers have marched to their deaths to a song. I do know why most religions depend on singing or canorous chant. It's how God reminds us that even a superstition created millennia ago can always construct a more hospitable home.

WILL OF A PRINCE

"Prince died without a will . . ."
—*NEW YORK TIMES*

To the first song I wrote at seven years old
on my father's forbidden piano, I leave
the sacred key of audacity. I don't know
who will press their hungering

across their own set of onyx & ivory
in a generation or two or three, but to all
those millions of little hands, I offer up my fingers
like two willows in a breeze.

To the legacy of sound, I bequeath
these eardrums I must now take off like tantric jewels,
lustrous & shimmering with funk. To all the controversy
I created in my lifetime, I leave no apologies

& thirty-eight other albums.
To the wild doves who taught me
mine sees what blinds
trapped inside a diamond, I leave

a castle of psychedelic stained-glass windows, flung open
for fluttering *you,* even in the wintertime. To my life-
long relationship with God, I offer the faithful
dot of my naked body bowing under the great curvaceous mystery
        of His question mark.

To Minneapolis, I leave a legion of little Northside Mozarts
air-guitaring their way up the charts
(& in the meantime hooping all summer with two rusty nets & a long-range
        three-point sunset).
To the more politically outspoken role some wished I'd played, I leave

my charismatic gaze & melodic sashays up & down the stage.
To the hip bones I nearly ground to dust with splits & pirouettes,
I leave a half acre of broken stilettos. To my love
of rock, I leave my penchant to pop like a super boss-

a nova; to my obsession with funk, my repertoire
of gospel & opera. To my reverence for big band jazz,
I leave all the instruments I never learned how to play professionally or for fun,
which, of course, y'all know was none.

To my modesty, I don't leave shit.
To my spontaneity, I lay at your feet the lassoing curiosity of my vocal cords.
To my falsetto, you dirty little girl, I unclothe my loveliest closet baritone.
To my androgyneity, you angel in a demon's dream,

I leave a glyph pointing down to both question & answer.
To Love,
I thank you, though you didn't always treat me so well,
I still love you & always will.

To the deer who fog my window just before dawn,
I leave my muse asleep at the piano.
To all the verbena, clematis & lavender in the world,
I give back with ample interest all the purple I ever borrowed.

To my race, I leave behind the pop apartheid of the '80s.
To joy, I give all my rococo beats, guitar riffs cataclysmic,
jabby synths & shiver-inducing screams. To melancholy,
I bequeath a slew of haunting coos & creamy soulful feasts.

To fate, I leave all my most buoyant bass lines—funkadelic from outer space.
I never really believed in the material world, so to it, I leave
all the magic that wherever I played, I always left entire & sizzling on stage.
To my sincerity, I bestow a pimp-strut promenade.

To my swag, I offer my two-pears-in-a-plastic-bag ass cheeks,
sometimes minus the bag. I know, honey I know,
in spiritual matters sometimes I had to knock on your door.
To all my pronouncements on morality, I leave a thousand free

concerts in *my* home, to which anyone, & I mean *anyone,* was always welcome.
To my final days, I offer up a song I wrote
but myself don't yet know how to hear, a soul
that my whole life kept changing its composer.

To all the godfathers & godmothers
yet to be born & bear the weight of theirs, I leave
this cosmic, contradictory, sacrilegious chord.
Go on, play it if you dare.

It shrieks true through my navel & just 4 U
I left the door wide open.

SUMMER OPEN WINDOW

Wait why
Is that singing

I usually love
So bad

Tonight from the Sober House next door?
O.K.,

Of course. Their damp
Piano has newly

Been tuned.

SUNDAY LISTENING

"A bee performs the waggle dance when she wants to inform other bees of a nectar source. . . . During the waggle, she dances a figure-eight pattern, with a straight 'walk' in between the loops and a sporadic fluttering of her wings . . ."
    —NOVA

All morning, our fourteen-month-old
expounds on the songs

other animals have abandoned long ago
to become human. Babbling

coos and clucks in a medley, punctuated
by three lung-lustrous sighs.

What in *our* world is she saying?
From the leaves above us, invisible

birds accompany her
meandering soprano,

or is it the reverse? My guess is
it doesn't matter at this Sunday picnic

brunch in the shade of a poplar
or maple or is it an ash—I admit I'm most-

ly ignorant of the nomenclature
of trees, wild syntax

of grass, weeds, planets, beetles,
spores, and so many dragonflies!—

each with a language as baffling as my own
daughter's lexical singsong, comprised

of five or six tones of squeal,
eight different hums, a funny trill. Sometimes

it's all I can do to lean in
despite the breeze and blossoms

bowing and bursting
before me to see

this little heart-shaped mouth
so hard at work with both

her mother's and father's lips;
all four grandparents' taste buds;

all eight great-
grandparents' glottises in one,

and so on, all the way back
beyond any human

utterance, or civilization's
sibilance, plosives, or diphthongs—far

to the very earliest honeybee's
waggling hind

shuck and swivel of a belly
so ecstatically determined

despite her hive's buzzing din
to share the source

of a newfound nectar
on the lazy side of the wind.

BLACKBERRY STAINS STILL ALIVE IN THE FUTURE

My life is a smokestack.

                Dreams burn here all night.

Though the factory has since become a village of condominiums.

Meanwhile, emus in our garden

                        bake savory pies, filled with

Silage and coke from my late father's mouth.

                            Or did I abandon all

His best hopes for my life too eagerly, like the funeral

Flowers we had to leave behind?

                      What does it matter now?

In that old, sad town, there is a rusty zoo with

Creatures who possess broken blackberries for eyes.

There, the young ignore the old, and the old can only hope—

Among all passing stains, none ever wanders back from the horizon.

3 A.M. REHABILITATION

Rockabying our inconsolable newborn,
My pinkie the live bait her mouth just won't take,
I understand certain bad things I've done.
Nothing unspeakable, beyond time's power
To heal the gentler temperaments deep inside a heart.
But if there were a Prison for Insensitive Behavior, I might have served
A year or two.
                    Meanwhile, somewhere far away
Inside steel reinforced walls, another kind of father
                                        Shifts in his seat, sweating
The iron file baked into the bunny-shaped birthday cake he's brought,
Waiting for another kind of daughter
                In stripes to be buzzed out, pick up the phone, and smile.

THE SCHOONER

Farther inside this long bar near Lake and Hiawatha, they burn
Over beers in the dark, these men and two women, creaking
Fatigue on stools, dead drunk. It is summer. The sun a cancer.
The God of Silence today has called a quorum of minor gods who have created
And destroyed whole voices and lives. Where else to go
If all you want is to drink to the sound of clearing throats?

The verdict is in. Men of Hope shall be resigned to steal quiet turns vomiting.
Stunned prairie horse spirits surviving civilization.
Some come with money to grin through a second happy hour.
Others doze after one shot, like a bullet from behind. Teetering
Faded tattoos over silver threads of drool. The bartender
Collects a pile of quarters and dimes, picks out the lint.
Sally, an old white lady with a pink mohawk, cackles in her Army coat.
Sometimes life splatters like an artist with no training or vision.

*

Imagine stick figures walking through a world of rich, seeping colors.
Smiling, they inhabit donated baggy denim and flannel. One fermenting
    soul gets stabbed
For singing another's karaoke song. One human being in red sparkly pumps
Gets attacked then imprisoned for being too male or female for another's
    liking.
Meth once in the popcorn machine. Pull tabs rigged. Meat raffle rigged.
Every bar at 3 p.m. is a ship deck after the typhoon.
You're still alive is enough cause for celebration!

**

I could tell you I drank there because
The attic I lived in had no air-conditioner. I could say
It was a period when I was unemployed or lived only two blocks away; my
    father stalked his cancer, gun in hand; I just liked fruit flies.
I remember: a novel in progress about space garbage

And how on Super Sunday and the Fourth of July they put out celery and
     pizzas for free on the duct-taped pinball machine.
But, really, it was the *water lilies*—how they'd reappear and disappear
In the stiff, late-night breeze, buzzing
Above crushed cans and condoms in wet leaves, on each slow stumble home.
One, a fuzzy planet. Another, a troubled century.
A third, just a lazy-eyed junkie on the block named LeNay.

***

A man steps into a bar, takes a seat among an old Norwegian, a Somali,
And an Indian. There is no punch line.
Instead, it's like anti-church. Or descending the Grand Canyon.
Only at bedrock can you look up
And witness all the lavish gradations of loss. The world
Is full of missionaries. Only the Angel of Death
Can kiss and hand you the knife
You'll need to carve out your own capacity to be happy.

So I did.

SPACE

When our Babygirl was born, a space
inaccessible inside me suddenly began to breathe.

One day, I know, her rasps and purrs,
                                oceanic to the core,
will have floated beyond more caverns than my eyes could ever behold.

There, she's already lost in some labyrinth
rehearsing a spell against dragons. Now
an adolescent, closing thoughtlessly
her door, hazy
                between a wild crown of hair and phone's glow.

Now a grown woman, wiping away tears of joy
or pain, or both,
                    I can't tell because the bellowing that consumes
is so vastly her own,
                no one, not I, nor her mother, nor a future lover

could lead her by the hand to see the stars in such a deep or shallow well.

But for now she's still just a baby
of course,
            and I have my palms, my forearms, and two more nursery rhymes
to soothe such fast-fluttering lungs.

For now my voice can still crack
and loll with the sweet news of hers—spun
inside one
            lit chrysalis of very early mornings.

GARDEN LESSON

A young child asks his mother what happened to all their houseplants' parents; did she have to kill the mothers and fathers to take and pot their children—and, if so, did they scream?

He has kept silent all week, during which his family has toured home after home in search of one they can finally live in.

He has stared wordless, in these houses for sale, at the few living plants, each whispering, *This too could happen to you, abandoned, uprooted from somewhere far, to end up here on a windowsill or a counter, hopelessly alone.*

It was the last trip to the garden store, its greenhouse shelves crammed with plants and flowers like sad animals at a zoo, that finally compelled the boy's need to know—what had happened to all the plants' brothers and sisters and cousins and family members surely still alive in the jungle or rain forest?

The boy's mother, a refugee and immigrant, shakes a rinsed sprig of fresh basil at the sink, and kneels to explain to her troubled son: *We are all houseplants and animals to God, and one day when it's time, forces will take each of us from our homes and families to live among others unlike us, in new towns, over rivers and mountains and seas, through decades of stories of who we once thought ourselves to be. This is why seeds endure, and soil is everywhere.*

Of course the boy doesn't understand.

The woman kisses him on the forehead, then sends him out to their apartment's vacant lot for some dandelion greens and perilla, lollygagging in a late-summer breeze with the fennel and thyme. None has a clue what is about to happen.

PINK LADY'S ANTENNA RECEIVES THE FUTURE

Atop my shoulders, she trots me like a Clydesdale.

Pink pussy hats & hearts, 100,000, thronging the Capitol.

When it begins to rain, some head for shelter,
Most chant even louder.
                                Is she o.k.? I shout.

Bridget momentarily lowers our umbrella & takes a picture:
Between pink hat & pink scarf,
                            Babygirl's tongue, extended skyward like a stamen.

DARK MATTERS

They eat vegetables from soil
nacre-black of fossils and shale;
soil in a garden kitty-corner from a church

whose headstones fade eons younger
than the souls chewing tonight
its fresh arugula, chives, perilla, and kale at a table

with stories, mirin, and a little salt.
See how they glow
in bed, beneath

down and cotton covers, amid wood
cut by machines and calloused hands;
steel, aluminum, and iron mined

from a necropolis of meteorites.
No wonder they comprehend so little,
these creatures—humans, let's call them,

germinating in this under-soil
of heaven or samsara or cheon
where all ancestors' dreams run free or wild.

Down below, in earth-dark sleep,
a light flickers and the Golgi apparatus
begins playing like a projector

on the walls of lung and brain cells
inside these roiling beings.
The characters change,

but the plot is always the same:
creatures born,
grow, maybe reproduce,

then get reabsorbed
into dark matter between
expanding and contracting stars.

And the whole time—
one's epidermis seeking warmth
in another's stratosphere.

BABYGIRL LEARNS TO TAKE A TRIP AROUND VENUS

You could say flowers plant humans in the middle
of their sometimes flamboyant, mostly tranquil lives.
Take these violets we stroll past each day along the sidewalk, leaves
scalloped, sepals half-concealed like they know what is coming.
See how our Babygirl greets each face-to-face, nose bobbing, tongue
tip hovering over the anthers like a bee. She doesn't care
this diminutive flower contains hydrocarbonic terpenes to temporarily
desensitize her olfactory receptors. Does not know
one spring not a mile away, as violets bloomed, a Hmong family of four
    from Frogtown
bought the house behind my landlord's, and the next week I overheard
two white neighbors mumbling: like dandelions more would come
because you know how the Hmong breed like weeds.
Not a word of the apartment complex down the way,
mostly black, that nearby gear-supply factory's history. Or
the boarding house a block south, its men
with secret shifts surrounding all the taquerias up and down Lake Street.
Or the Little Earth Native American housing projects four blocks north of
    the Pioneer and Soldiers Memorial Cemetery.
And nothing of the Scandinavians and other Europeans—all the mice,
hemlock, and smallpox stowed away on their ships.

                              All Babygirl understands is violets
taste like vanilla and wintergreen. And if she holds my hand, we can cross
the street to visit the empty seedpods, wild plantain, and clover.
And when we cross back home, she needs to greet her best purple-blue friends
    all over again.
You could say their spirits were always here;
that this common, flirtatious flower adored by Napoleon and used by Venus
to batter and bruise prettier goddesses
furtively fans its admirers.

                          But it'd only be half true.
Take the African violets on our porch—aka *Saintpaulias*
after Baron Walter von Saint Paul, a middling colonial
administrator who in 1892 *discovered* the flowering blue wild on a rocky ledge
in the Usambara Mountains of Tanzania, therein initiating their mass
    cultivation to the West.

Maybe all flowers have an imperializing function.

If not to cover up the stench, to beautify all the graves.

Part Korean, Irish, Ukrainian, French, German, and Jew,

O Babygirl, I want to believe your future is an open field of glorious weeds
and wildflowers,

not a legacy of granite statues, strip malls, and parking ramps.

You're only two years old, with not fifteen world-soaked words, but someday

when you can stay up late enough to gaze at the moon, instead

I'll take you on a long walk through our Milky Way.

I'll advise ignoring all the categories, all the nomenclature: Kuiper Belt,
Cygnus Constellation, Fornax Cluster.

Look, I'll say, listen to that far bouquet of stars, its pulse

like an autumn copse of quaking aspens.

I'll insist: in this infinite universe, no one cares: *Where are you from? What
are you?*

It may not be true.

But I'll say it anyway: far in your future,

all will recognize a human being when they encounter one.

And if they don't—

as with violets, red maples, stinging nettles, even Jupiter's loneliest moon—

you'll still know what to do.

END OF THE WORLD

At *the end of the world* when the last human was gone, a trillion-times-a-
trillion plants lived on—each a radiant angel, offering beauty, oxygen,
and sometimes fruit, expecting nothing for its own life in return.

Not a single plant ever craved human shape.

None pitied or tried to redeem anything fallen.

Some learned to thrive on methane, radiation, cosmic rays, three centuries
of dust coating the atmosphere at *the end of the world*.

Each simply lived as it had always done, in concert with its kin for a day
or a million millennia, morphing at times but essentially existing the
same way.

If any had wings—green or red, ultraviolet or brown—few attempted to
get very far, preferring to twirl and pirouette in the wind.

None questioned why it had been struck by lightning or its grandfather
had been starved, or, if endowed with bark, why it was soggily diseased
or scorched, why in old age it had lost its petals, needles, hypanthia, or
a limb.

In fact, not long after *the end of the world,* there were more plants than at the
beginning or at any point in the middle. Plants shattering greenhouse
windows; plants bursting though the walls of industrial office parks,
cracking concrete, engulfing nuclear reactors and skyscrapers in vines
and foliage like hair.

Afterward, when the sun finally did cool, long after the last plant slowly
withered and that largest molecule of all called *Earth* disappeared back
into dark matter—somewhere, *something*—still dreaming in an ancient
poetry of chemical energy, knitting together one muon, gluon, boson at
a time; midway between the octaves of carbon, chlorophyll, and
ribosome; on a wavelength of rapture—longed to meet its closest

alien neighbor, and so, robust, technologically advanced, and wise,
eventually arrived from a great journey to slide and burrow and one day
reemerge from its battered hull

Then peer around.

ON A DESERT HIGHWAY

The shaman wore long white sleeves rippling &
Minuscule in the bone-dry distance.
                               I jerked & righted the wheel
Plying invisible waves of hot sea
Always a moment just before the immediate future.

These warped slurs of air made of decades, centuries, a few
Seconds, who knows how speed/time/thermodynamics work when you're
    seated in air-
Conditioned comfort.
                     In my reverie, soon I forgot
I should have crashed into the first shining spirit hours before.
The mind itself a wobbly mirage on an endless road laid out before you.
                                          Past midnight,
Momentarily dozing at seventy-nine miles per hour,
                                   A second shaman's white
Sleeves fluttered far ahead in the headlights, this one
Scattering yellow tulips from a basket like cake frosting on the fillet of asphalt.
                                        A third wearing red
                     Scallop shells of grief
Still favors my raw primary years in sleep—
Always asking hoarsely for a new face to wear to parties, church, shopping
    malls, funerals.

Whatever age I am right now,
Whatever degree of luminosity
In a dream or memory I have not yet had,
Let me say:
          I will always acknowledge & race toward your shipwrecked souls—

Far beyond the blood vessels behind my lids,
Past even those frightening cacti of a million cochleas,
Swooshed into that amniotic zone
                     Where once we all soared, naked & glowing.

READING IN BED IS LIKE HEAVEN

"There is a lamp on my table. And the house is in the book."
—EDMOND JABÈS

And now I see it's not the meanings I loved most
demolishing each labyrinth flooded with belief,

but the quandaries—
                    arrived like curious spirits
on the precipice of trauma or slumber—
                              Worlds inside words
paginated & unspooling
a knotted core of images.

Like a strange animal breathing
the amber linen of an old book on rare gems

in search of a new home to die in.

IN THIS ZOO EVERYTHING IS IN DRAG

A shining school of green fish moves in unison with a far harem of zebras.

Binoculars dangle around elk necks.

Like others here, I wander in and out of languages, religions, genders, political denominations, bodies, nomenclatures, eons, origins.

Death messages like leukemia and lottery tickets nip at the legs of experts and dilettantes passing by.

I am a microbe. I am an infant sea slug. I am a slunk homunculus blink-filled, shuffling wingtips.

On the marred heads of chimpanzees, moss and lichen have been speaking in tongues for generations and will continue to entertain themselves, creating whole cultures and wars and jokes and recipes and metaphors into the next supereon's star systems.

Meanwhile, a semitruck full of marigolds just swooshed past the woman who delivers our daily beets and porridge and meat mauled by the hot orders of subatomic particles wildly behemoth to the minions who praise our shadows whenever we so much as sneeze.

Nothing alive snug in its name. Even art—like a great cargo ship veering starboard midsea—has at some indeterminate point in the night become inverted and backward.

Sometimes it seems to make sense. Something with your tastes and marrow and winter coat leads you to a place where no one even remotely like you has ever been.

The soul, pure intuition.

Here: God is wood. Those creatures pushing a cart of diamonds and tears up a sloping hill are not weeping but singing. God is stone. Those other creatures returning down from their elaborate architectures of dirt are smaller, happier, more fearless and unburdened than those who just barely made it in. God is water.

If you open your eyes too wide, you'll have to crawl out of your oldest nucleolus to find the next hole, and so on, until the most suffocating notion of all: there are no more holes.

And yet, you can't help but keep asking others approaching on the path for the time.

Some days, when the weather is exceptionally fine, the most senior zoo-keeper will stop and confess an account of a recent breach in the outer wall, and then, and only then, might you experience a tumultuous intimation that for too long you have all been donning the wrong insignias, vesting your dreams on but the simplest amoeba's technology.

WATER IN LOVE

How to love like water loves
when it's impossible to even taste
all the ghostly sediments
each time you take a sip

Impossible to savor
the salt in your blood
the light and island shorelines
in each living cell

When even the plainest mouthful
tastes more of you than you of it

Sweetest of absences
that frees in wave after wave
debris of thought like the dead,
the drowned, the vanished, and yet
sails your lips
on a voyage toward another's, plying
all luck and regret

Worship, splash, guzzle, or forget
It clears any difference
Stone washer and mountain dissolver
that will
outlive us, even the memory of
all any eyes touched

Wasp and cactus in a desert
Comet through outer space
Sleep among all the cloud-shepherds' children

A love so perpetually current
it doesn't care that you love
without even knowing you love
what you couldn't survive
three days without

How to love like that: wild
dream-sparkler and inmost virtuoso
of every snowflake

Wise, ebullient, and generous
as the rain

Deepest of miracles
for a time
borrowing and replenishing
a self
overflowing with fate

NOTES

"Halfway to a New Home" chronicles formative episodes in my mother's, Ae-hyung Lee's, history. Ethnically Korean, she was born in China, where her family lived until, when she was very young, they were forced to flee, first during the Second Sino-Japanese War (1937–45), then once again during the Pacific War (1941–45). Eventually, they resettled a third time in what is now commonly known as North Korea (near where her parents had been born), but then again, as refugees, were uprooted during the Korean War (1950–53), fleeing this time to the recently created (and soon to be militarily contested over) South Korea.

"Powderhorn" refers to artist Michael Hoyt's Rolling Revelry project (2013): a series of bicycle- and pedestrian-focused events intent on bringing mobile, publicly projected karaoke to city streets and bike paths.

"Ode to the Poems of Any Small Nation" refers to the Koryŏ dynasty (935–1392 CE). The Western name for Korea is derived from Koryŏ (고려).

The article referred to in the epigraph for "Super-Insensitive Species" was published in *Scientific American,* July 5, 2013.

"Centrifuge" alludes to the Bình Hòa Massacre, which was reportedly conducted by South Korean military forces (neocolonial allies of the United States during the war in Vietnam) in either October or December of 1966 in the Bình Hòa village in the Quảng Ngãi province of what was then known as South Vietnam. An estimated 403 people were killed, mostly the elderly, children, and women—twenty-one of whom were reported to have been pregnant.

"Gwangju" takes its title from the name of the sixth-largest city in South Korea, located in the South Jeolla province. From May 18–27, 1980, an estimated 606 people died at the hands of South Korean troops during a civil uprising against the military dictatorship of Chun Doo-hwan.

"Postelection Poem, November" alludes to the November 8, 2016, presidential election in which business mogul and reality-TV star Donald J. Trump was elected the forty-fifth president of the United States of America.

Section five of "Colonizing a Different Sun" refers to the Japanese colonial occupation of Korea (1910–45).

Section six of "Colonizing a Different Sun" is taken from a play I wrote, *Glow* (2003), which explored the intergenerationally complex lives of clones. The play was originally presented at the New York Theatre Workshop in 2004, followed by public performances at Mu Performing Arts and the National Asian American Theater Conference at the Guthrie Theater in Minneapolis in 2008.

The article referred to in the epigraph for "Sunday Listening" was published at pbs.org on January 4, 2000.

"The Schooner" refers to a fatal stabbing outside the Schooner Tavern on June 5, 2011, in Minneapolis. In the case, Chrishaun "CeCe" McDonald, an African American, transgender woman, was charged with second-degree murder for stabbing Dean Schmitz, a white man with an extensive criminal history, directly in the heart after the latter's group taunted the former's companions with racist and homophobic slurs. Before the fatal stabbing, a woman smashed a glass in McDonald's face, which later required eleven stitches.

"Pink Lady's Antenna Receives the Future" was written after the January 21, 2017, Women's March, a worldwide protest.

"Dark Matters" refers to *cheon* (천), a Korean, Confucian-based concept of the afterlife, influenced variously by Taoism, Buddhism, and animism.

Ed Bok Lee is a fiscal year 2014 recipient of an Artist Initiative grant from the Minnesota State Arts Board. This activity is made possible by the voters of Minnesota through a grant from the Minnesota State Arts Board, thanks to a legislative appropriation by the Minnesota State Legislature, and by a grant from the National Endowment for the Arts.

MINNESOTA
STATE ARTS BOARD

ART WORKS.

National
Endowment
for the Arts
arts.gov

LITERATURE
is not the same thing as
PUBLISHING

Coffee House Press began as a small letterpress operation in 1972 and has grown into an internationally renowned nonprofit publisher of literary fiction, essay, poetry, and other work that doesn't fit neatly into genre categories.

Coffee House is both a publisher and an arts organization. Through our *Books in Action* program and publications, we've become interdisciplinary collaborators and incubators for new work and audience experiences. Our vision for the future is one where a publisher is a catalyst and connector.

Funder Acknowledgments

Coffee House Press is an internationally renowned independent book publisher and arts nonprofit based in Minneapolis, MN; through its literary publications and *Books in Action* program, Coffee House acts as a catalyst and connector—between authors and readers, ideas and resources, creativity and community, inspiration and action.

Coffee House Press books are made possible through the generous support of grants and donations from corporations, state and federal grant programs, family foundations, and the many individuals who believe in the transformational power of literature. This activity is made possible by the voters of Minnesota through a Minnesota State Arts Board Operating Support grant, thanks to the legislative appropriation from the Arts and Cultural Heritage Fund. Coffee House also receives major operating support from the Amazon Literary Partnership, the Jerome Foundation, McKnight Foundation, Target Foundation, and the National Endowment for the Arts (NEA). To find out more about how NEA grants impact individuals and communities, visit www.arts.gov.

Coffee House Press receives additional support from the Elmer L. & Eleanor J. Andersen Foundation; the David & Mary Anderson Family Foundation; Bookmobile; Fredrikson & Byron, P.A.; Dorsey & Whitney LLP; the Fringe Foundation; Kenneth Koch Literary Estate; the Knight Foundation; the Matching Grant Program Fund of the Minneapolis Foundation; Mr. Pancks' Fund in memory of Graham Kimpton; the Schwab Charitable Fund; Schwegman, Lundberg & Woessner, P.A.; the U.S. Bank Foundation; and VSA Minnesota for the Metropolitan Regional Arts Council.

The Publisher's Circle of Coffee House Press

Publisher's Circle members make significant contributions to Coffee House Press's annual giving campaign. Understanding that a strong financial base is necessary for the press to meet the challenges and opportunities that arise each year, this group plays a crucial part in the success of Coffee House's mission.

Recent Publisher's Circle members include many anonymous donors, Suzanne Allen, Patricia A. Beithon, the E. Thomas Binger & Rebecca Rand Fund of the Minneapolis Foundation, Andrew Brantingham, Robert & Gail Buuck, Louise Copeland, Jane Dalrymple-Hollo, Mary Ebert & Paul Stembler, Kaywin Feldman & Jim Lutz, Chris Fischbach & Katie Dublinski, Sally French, Jocelyn Hale & Glenn Miller, the Rehael Fund-Roger Hale/Nor Hall of the Minneapolis Foundation, Randy Hartten & Ron Lotz, Dylan Hicks & Nina Hale, William Hardacker, Randall Heath, Jeffrey Hom, Carl & Heidi Horsch, the Amy L. Hubbard & Geoffrey J. Kehoe Fund, Kenneth & Susan Kahn, Stephen & Isabel Keating, Kenneth Koch Literary Estate, Cinda Kornblum, Jennifer Kwon Dobbs & Stefan Liess, Lambert Family Foundation, Lenfestey Family Foundation, Sarah Lutman & Rob Rudolph, the Carol & Aaron Mack Charitable Fund of the Minneapolis Foundation, George & Olga Mack, Joshua Mack & Ron Warren, Gillian McCain, Malcolm S. McDermid & Katie Windle, Mary & Malcolm McDermid, Sjur Midness & Briar Andresen, Maureen Millea Smith & Daniel Smith, Peter Nelson & Jennifer Swenson, Enrique & Jennifer Olivarez, Alan Polsky, Marc Porter & James Hennessy, Robin Preble, Alexis Scott, Ruth Stricker Dayton, Jeffrey Sugerman & Sarah Schultz, Nan G. & Stephen C. Swid, Kenneth Thorp in memory of Allan Kornblum & Rochelle Ratner, Patricia Tilton, Joanne Von Blon, Stu Wilson & Melissa Barker, Warren D. Woessner & Iris C. Freeman, and Margaret Wurtele.

For more information about the Publisher's Circle and other ways
to support Coffee House Press books, authors, and activities,
please visit www.coffeehousepress.org/pages/support
or contact us at info@coffeehousepress.org.

ED BOK LEE is the author of *Whorled* (Coffee House Press) and a recipient of a 2012 American Book Award and the Minnesota Book Award in Poetry. Lee is the son of North and South Korean emigrants—his mother originally a refugee from what is now North Korea and his father raised during the Japanese colonial period and Korean War in what is now South Korea. Lee grew up in South Korea, North Dakota, and Minnesota and was educated there and later on both U.S. coasts and in Russia, South Korea, and Kazakhstan. He teaches at Metropolitan State University in Saint Paul, Minnesota. Other honors include the Asian American Literary Award (Members' Choice Award) and a PEN Open Book Award.

Mitochondrial Night was designed by
Bookmobile Design & Digital Publisher Services.
Text is set in Arno Pro.